Don't Eat your Slime

Incredible Experiments for Curious Kids!

Mad Marc (Wileman)

ISBN 978-1-4716-5038-3

'Don't Eat Your Slime' is the book that I
wish I'd had when I was a kid!
Let's get started!
Yours,

Mad Marc

Founder, Sublime Science

CONTENTS:

The Intro Stuff:

The Experiments:

WARNING: (legal type stuff)

WARNING No 1:

You and your child may get excited about science!

WARNING No 2:

All these experiments are reasonably low risk however things can (and will) sometimes go wrong! Please follow the instructions carefully, make sure you have an adult on hand to help out and note that I or Sublime Science expressly disclaim all liability for any occurrence, including, but not limited to, damage, injury or death which might arise as consequences of the use of any experiment(s) listed or described here. Therefore, you assume all the liability and use these science experiment projects at your own risk!

Mad Marc Says: Have Fun! Get a sane and sensible adult to help you - but get stuck in - have a go and enjoy doing it!

INTRODUCTION:

What's it all about?

In short - This is the book that I dreamt about when I was a kid! A 'how to' guide of awesome experiments that you can do with stuff that you've already got!

Who wrote this thing?

Hi! I'm Mad Marc (Marc Wileman on more sensible occasions!) and I founded Sublime Science to show children just how awesome science can be! I've got a First Class Masters Degree in Physics (Universities of Nottingham & Toronto) and have been a Professional Science Communicator (maker of slime & launcher of rockets!) across the UK, Canada and Australia too!

I'm proud to have been featured by the BBC, ITV & The Telegraph and to have worked with the British Science Association and National Science Museum. I've even received a congratulatory letter from 10 Downing Street! - Enough about me - Let's get started!

1. Slimetastic Fun

There are so many ways to make slime. With this one you won't need to go in search of crazy chemicals, you probably already have everything that you need. Ready?... then let's get started!

(P.S. - We make a different slime (our favourite) at our live events)

What do I need?

- Food Colouring
- Cornflour ("normal" flour won't do the trick)
- 2 Cups
- Water
- Maybe some kitchen roll to clean up!

How do I do it?

STEP1 - Add a few drops of food colouring to half a cup of water (real slime is always green!)

STEP2 - Fill another cup one quarter of the way with cornflour

STEP3 - SLOWLY! Add a few drops of the water at a time to the cornflour and mix it all together with your hand.

STEP4 - Keep adding a few drops at a time, then stirring the slime until you get a slimy mess! If you add too much water you'll get something too watery! If that happens add some more cornflour.

STEP5 - Enjoy your slime!!

What's going on?
The beautiful slime is known as a "Non-Newtonian fluid". That just means it's not really a liquid or a solid (it's kind of both and kind of neither).

More Fun Please! - Experiment like a real scientist!
- Experiment with your slime. Try prodding it with your finger quickly and it will feel hard like a solid or if you pour it across your hands slowly it will feel like a liquid.
- Try making different coloured slimes.
- Try and make the 'perfect slime' with different amounts of water!

IMPORTANT! - When you are done with your slime, not for some time I'm sure! - Don't pour it down the drain. The slime will separate back into cornflour and water and this can clog the pipes. Just wrap it in some paper and put it in the bin. (If you can bring yourself to!)

2. An Exploding Fountain - (The mints and cola thing)

One of the most fun (and messy) experiments ever! Just be sure to do it in plenty of space and find out the science behind it too.

WARNING! - This Experiment MUST be done Outside!

What do I need?
- A 2 litre bottle of fizzy drink (any will do!)
- Mints
- A cardboard toilet roll
- Pen, scissors & sticky tape

How do I do it?

STEP1 - First we need to make a mints dropper!

- Cut the toilet roll (or other card) so it can be rolled round into a tube that's just a bit wider than one of your mints!
- Tape the tube together
- Push a pen/pencil through the tube - that's the firing pin
- Fill the tube from the top with mints (7 is perfect!)

STEP2 - Take your dropper (loaded with mints) and lemonade to an outdoor space where you can make a mess.

STEP3 - Make sure you're OUTSIDE, have a final check... attach the tube to the bottle and then pull the pen back - This will explode into a messy fountain so quickly get well back!

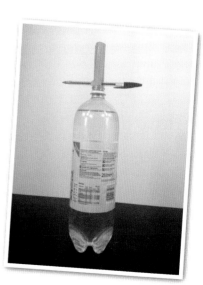

What's going on?

The bubbling fountain of lemonade that's (hopefully not) just drenched you is one of the world's most fun experiments. It's also one that's badly explained (even by scientists!).

The lemonade bottle is packed full of carbon dioxide, that's why it starts fizzing as soon as you take the lid off! The bubbles form on tiny scratches and scuffs on the inside of the container known as nucleation points. The lemonade will fizz away for a while and then, once all the carbon dioxide has come out, go flat.

The mints just speed this up - instead of the bubbles coming out over a few hours it all comes out in a few seconds! The surface of a mint is the perfect place for bubbles to form - which is why they are the 'magic' ingredient!

3. Let's Make Some Lava!

Ok, so it's not the 'real' lava from volcanoes but it's still pretty awesome, completely safe and I bet that you've already got everything that you need! Let's get cracking!

WARNING: Parents, this may remind you of the lava lamps of days gone by and make you feel very nostalgic!

What do I need:
- Vegetable oil
- A glass or transparent cup
- Food colouring
- Salt

How do I do it?

STEP1 - Fill your glass just over half full with water and add a good few drops of food colouring.

STEP2 - Pour some vegetable oil into your cup. It will soon settle and form a layer of oil on top of the water.

STEP3 - Sprinkle a good dollop of salt into your cup to start making your lava!

What's Going on?

First of all the oil will settle out to form a layer on top of the water because it's lighter (technically it's less dense) so it floats on top.

When you add a dollop of salt it's heavier (more dense) so it sinks through the oil and water pulling some of the vegetable oil down with it.

13

Next, the salt will start to dissolve into the water. This will free up the oil and as it's lighter (less dense) it will rise back up and float on top of the water.

Oil and water don't mix (scientists like to say that oil is hydrophobic) and so the oil stays together as a blob as it rises through the water - giving you your very own cup full of lava!

More Fun Please! - Experiment like a real scientist!

- Try different types of oil, olive, sunflower, etc. and see how it changes the lava.
- How long will the lamp work for? Can you just keep adding salt forever?
- What's the best shaped container to make the perfect lava lamp? Tall and thin? Short and fat? Experiment and find out!

4. The Legendary Volcano!

Our lava might have been homemade but the real stuff comes right out of volcanos! Let's have a go at making our own volcano with a twist!

TOP TIP: An awesome extra idea is to decorate your volcano so it looks realistic. Use paper mache and paint and all the rest! Here I just want to show you how to make sure it works - so your volcano erupts with a bang!

What do I need:

- Washing up liquid
- White vinegar
- Cup or glass
- Baking soda
- Spoon

How do I do it?

STEP1 - Fill your glass just over half full with water, add 3 tea spoons full of baking soda and give it a good stir until most of the baking soda dissolves.

STEP2 - Add a good squirt of washing up liquid into the cup and once again give it a stir.

STEP3 - Make sure your volcano is in the kitchen or outside (or somewhere you don't mind making a mess).

STEP4 - Quickly pour in just under a quarter of a cup of vinegar and enjoy your very own volcanic eruption!

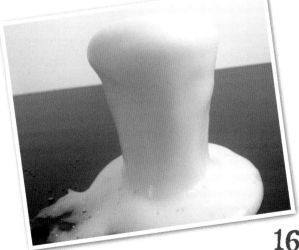

What's going on?

Congratulations - You just made your very own chemical reaction! Mixing the acid (vinegar) and the alkali (bicarbonate of soda) and releasing bubbles of carbon dioxide (CO_2). The washing up liquid is just there to trap those bubbles so it flows over the 'volcano' like real lava!

More Fun Please - Experiment like a real scientist!

- Try different amounts of both the vinegar and the baking soda and try and make the perfect eruption!
- If you're feeling brave (and are somewhere where it's OK to make a big mess) then add some red food colouring into your mixture, before you add the vinegar, to make it look just like real lava!

5. Magical Cup Drop!

Great science often looks like magic and it's time to learn a 'magic' trick that you can use to impress your friends! - Hopefully you'll be able to tell them how it works too!

WARNING: - Don't use anything too valuable! It takes a little practice to get this one working just right!

What do I need:

- A glass
- An egg (for the brave or a small ball or water balloon for the more cautious)
- A flat lid
- Another toilet roll

STEP1 - Half fill your glass with water - so it's nice and heavy and a soft landing for your falling balloon!

STEP2 - Stack the glass, lid, toilet roll and water balloon as shown.

STEP3 - Pull the lid out to the side in one fast but smooth motion. This may take a bit of practice.

STEP4 - Watch your friends gasp in amazement as the water balloon falls straight down into the water with a splash (but doesn't burst!)

What's going on?

This one is all to do with Newton's law of inertia!
That's just a law that says that an object will remain
at rest unless acted upon by another force. By
pulling the lid away quickly very little of the force
is transferred to the balloon and so it doesn't move
to the side. Then gravity does its work and pulls the
balloon down into the cup with a splash!

More Fun Please! - Experiment like a real scientist!

- First, practise with a water balloon to get the hang of it!
- Then, move up to a real egg and impress your friends!
- Finally, use a water balloon again and experiment by filling up with lots of water (so it's really big and heavy) and then use just a little water so it's small and light.

6. Make Your Own Flute - In Less Than 1 Minute!

Quite a few people learn to play a musical instrument (and that's amazing!) but very few learn to make one! We're about to make our very own straw flute and it'll only take a minute.

WARNING: - Make sure to have an adult help out with the scissors. Also, be careful, your pointy straw will be sharp. Finally make sure not to play your flute too often and drive your friends and family nuts!

What do I need:
- A straw (any old one will do)
- A pair of scissors

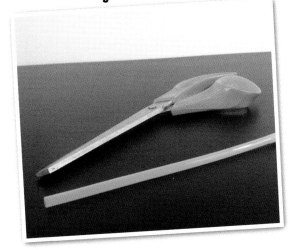

How do I do it?

STEP1 - Flatten the end of the straw (last 2 cm) down as much as possible with your nail.

STEP2 - Cut the end of the straw into a point as shown to the right.

STEP3 - Make sure the pointed end of the straw is open just a little bit (see bottom right image).

STEP4 - Blow gently through the pointed end of the straw. This can take a few minutes to get the hang of... Your straw will make a slightly rude sounding noise when you've cracked it! Good luck!

What's going on?

Every single noise in the whole world works the exact same way. From children talking when they shouldn't! To the best musicians in the world!

Whenever you hear a noise you know something must be vibrating (just another way of saying shaking). In this case it's the straw itself that's vibrating and making that beautiful noise.

More Fun Please! - Experiment like a real scientist!

- First of all, get the hang of playing your brand new instrument!
- Next up, see what happens to the sound when you make your straw shorter (just cut it shorter!).
- What happens when you blow it harder?
- Keep your eye out for thicker and thinner straws (when you're out and about) and see if you can hear a difference between them?

"The most exciting phrase to hear in science, the one that heralds the most discoveries, is not 'Eureka!' but 'That's funny...' - Isaac Asimov

7. The Sachet Submarine!

Make your very own submarine, that you control, inside a bottle! Let's get started!

What do I need:

- A screw top bottle full of water
- A sachet, tomato ketchup, brown sauce or in this case vinegar
- A glass of water
- Some Blue Tac

How do I do it?

STEP1 - Before we get going we need to make sure that our sachet floats just perfectly. Put the sachet into your glass of water and if it floats on top then just add a little Blue Tac until it 'just' floats. Just like the one in the image on the next page!
(You can also do this by trying a handful of sachets till you get one that's just right)

STEP2 - Pop the sachet inside the drinks bottle and screw the lid on tight!

STEP3 - Dive your sachet submarine into the depths simply be squeezing the side of the bottle.

STEP4 - Make your sachet submarine rise back up simply by releasing the bottle.

What's going on?

The little pocket of air inside the sachet means that it's lighter (less dense) and so it floats on top of the water. The Blue Tac is heavier (more dense) so adding a little bit means that the sachet barely floats.

When you squeeze the bottle this increases the pressure! This squashes that little pocket of air inside the sachet making it more dense so it starts to sink. When you let go of the bottle, the air inside the sachet spreads back out and the sachet gets bigger (making it less dense) and so your submarine rises back up to the surface!

NOTE: More dense just means heavier for the same size!

More Fun Please! - Experiment like a real scientist!

- Try different sachets and see what happens.
- What else could you use to make a submarine?
- Try only half filling the bottle with water, what happens?

8. Milktastic Fun!

You may well drink the white stuff every day but until now you probably never knew you could do an incredible science experiment with normal, everyday milk. Well, you do now! - So let's get started!

What do I need:
- A plate or bowl
- Washing up liquid
- Half a glass of milk
- Food colouring

How do I do it?

STEP1 - Pour your milk into your bowl or on to your plate until the surface is well covered

STEP2 - Add several drops of food colouring onto your milk.

STEP3 - Cover the end of your finger with washing up liquid (use a pen or pencil if you don't fancy getting messy.

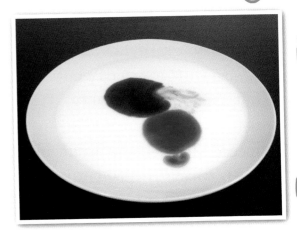

STEP4 - Dip your finger into the middle of your milk - Watch in amazement as the colours go flying off all over the place!

What's going on?

This one is all to do with something called surface tension - the force between the molecules on the surface of the milk.

Adding the washing up liquid reduces the surface tension of the milk. The rest of the milk still has the same surface tension as it did before and so pulls the milk outwards taking the food colouring with it! Cool, huh!

More Fun Please - Experiment like a real scientist!

- Is the type of milk important? Full fat? Skimmed?
- Which type of soap works best?

9. A Balloon Kebab Please!

A fantastic 'magic' trick you can use to impress your friends. There's some real science going on behind the fun, although this experiment has nothing to do with food I'm afraid!

WARNING: If you don't like the sound of balloons going bang then make sure you get this experiment right the first time! (Or cover up your ears!)

What do I need:
- A balloon (maybe a few, just in case you pop a couple!)
- A kebab skewer

How do I do it?

STEP1 - Once you've blown up and tied your balloon you'll be able to see a darker thicker section where the balloon skin is less stretched out? That's where we are going to push the skewer through!

STEP2 - Gently ease the skewer through the balloon, across to the other side!

STEP3 - Look closely for the darker circle of the balloon skin and very gently push the skewer through there!

STEP4 - You've done it! Admire your very own balloon kebab!

What's going on?

The moment you mention to someone that you're going to put a kebab skewer through a balloon most people cover up their ears! (and think you're mad!)

So, why doesn't the balloon pop? Notice how we're pushing the skewer through the darker parts of the balloon skin. These parts are not as stretched out and are still nice and elastic. So when you gently push the skewer through, the balloon can close up back round it, keep the air in and most importantly, not go bang!

More Fun Please! - Experiment like a real scientist!

- Try blowing your balloon up more (so it's bigger), does this make it more difficult?

10. Magical Movement?

There's just time for one final 'magic' trick to wow your friends with! A super simple but mysterious experiment to finish things up!

What do I need:

- A balloon
- An empty drinks can

WARNING: This experiment may mess up your hair!

How do I do it?

STEP1 - Blow up the balloon and rub it on your hair (or a woolly jumper) until you can feel the balloon pulling on your hair.

STEP2 - Check that you're ready. Once you've rubbed the balloon on your hair enough you should be able to stick it to the wall and it not fall down.

STEP3 - Lay a drinks can on its side on a flat smooth surface and put the balloon near to the can and then move it away in a pulling motion.

STEP3 - Watch in amazement as the can rolls after the balloon. Then stop being amazed and have a think about what's going on!

What's going on?

This experiment is all down to the wonders of static electricity! Rubbing the balloon on your head creates a build up of charge.

Then you put the balloon next to the wall and this charge is attracted to the opposite charge on the wall. This creates an attraction that is strong enough to overcome the gravity trying to pull the balloon down to the ground and that's what keeps it in place!

More Fun Please! - Experiment like a real scientist!

- How long will a balloon stay stuck to the wall for?
- Does it work with all types of drinks can?
- What happens if you only rub the balloon a little bit?
- Try using two balloons at the same time, what happens?

Thank You!

I hope you get as much fun out of this book as I did putting it together! Maybe even a little bit more!

I've had a blast making science fun and exciting for children and with this book the learning and discovery can go on all over the world, to places that Sublime Science can't get to.

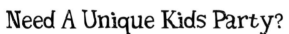

Need A Unique Kids Party?

Thanks for reading! We'd love to share even more awesome science!

Discover why the Sublime Science Party is Award-Winning and how it could make your child's next birthday unforgettable at:

www.SublimeScience.com